# DOLLEY MADISON

Dolley Madison was born in North Carolina in 1768. In her long gray Quaker dress and her gray bonnet tied under her chin, she went slowly through the forest to school. "Thee must remember to walk, not run. Thee must speak softly," her mother said. If Dolley wished secretly for bright colors, one day she would have them, for Dolley grew up and became the bride of James Madison, who would soon be President of the United States. Patricia Miles Martin writes with understanding and warmth of the little Quaker girl, and her role as first lady of our land.

A SEE AND READ
Beginning to Read Biography

# Dolley
# MADISON

by PATRICIA MILES MARTIN

Illustrated by UNADA

# G. P. Putnam's Sons    New York

# To my cousin, Gladys Armstrong

## See and Read Biographies of Famous Women

Dolley Madison
Sacajawea
Eleanor Roosevelt
Jacqueline Kennedy Onassis
Pocahontas
Marie Curie
Annie Sullivan

© 1967 by Patricia Miles Martin
All Rights Reserved
Published simultaneously in the Dominion of
Canada by Longmans Canada Limited, Toronto
*Library of Congress Catalog Card Number: 67-24163*
PRINTED IN THE UNITED STATES OF AMERICA
Fourth Impression
SBN: GB 399-60132-5

# DOLLEY MADISON

Seven year old Dolley Payne felt like
smiling, for she was walking along the
forest path on her way to school. It was
hard to keep her feet from running, when
she was so happy. It was hard to walk
slowly and quietly.

She had been born in 1768 in North Carolina. Her name was written in a big book in the Quaker Meeting House: "Dolley Payne."

She was the third child in a Quaker
family.

Her father moved his family to a
plantation in Virginia.

It was here that Dolley went to a school
for Quaker children. Her two older
brothers went with her. The school was in
a forest of pine trees, near a pleasant creek.

Like all Quaker girls, Dolley wore a long dress and her bonnet was tied under her chin.

She wore a white mask to keep the sun from her face. She wore white mittens on her hands.

"Thee must wear no bright colors," her mother had said. "And thee must remember to walk, not run. Thee must speak softly."

And so it was that Dolley walked demurely through the forest.

If she wished secretly for bright colors, she saw these in the wild flowers that grew near the path. If she wished for singing, she listened to the songs of the birds in the pine trees.

She remembered to speak softly.

14

Dolley lived in a very large house.

At night, the light from many candles twinkled in the black marble of great fireplaces.

Below stairs was a small hiding place that children like to think about.

Perhaps pirates had once been kept here.

Perhaps here, people had hidden from the Indians.

Outside was a kitchen with large pots over the fire in the fireplace.

Outside, too, were green fields and gardens that were well kept. Many slaves worked on this plantation.

Quakers did not believe that it was right to keep slaves, but by law, they could not be set free.

When Dolley was fourteen years old, the law was changed. Dolley's father called his slaves together. He wrote the papers that made them free.

Dolley's father could not stay on the plantation without slaves, and so he moved his family to a small house in Philadelphia.

In Philadelphia, Dolley saw wonderful new things.

In the store windows were hats with feathers and dresses with buttons and ribbons.

She heard the new sounds of the city.

In the day, there was the cry of the street vendor:

"Oysters — oysters —"

And at night, the town watchman called
the hour:

"Nine of the clock, and all is well!"

22

Dolley married a young Quaker, John Todd. They had two sons. In the autumn of 1793, yellow fever came to Philadelphia and quickly spread to every corner of the city. Many people died from this fever. Dolley's husband and their younger child lay dead.

Dolley and her little son, Payne, were left alone.

23

At this time, people in Philadelphia were
talking about a new capital city. It would
be in Washington. A Capitol building and
a President's Palace would be built there.

Now, the Congress of the new United
States met in Philadelphia.

Many important men came to the city:
Thomas Jefferson, Aaron Burr, James
Madison.

President George Washington was there.

James Madison and his tall friend,
Thomas Jefferson, were often seen walking
along the street, together.

Time passed.

One morning, Dolley wrote to her friend,
Eliza Collins.

"Thou must come to me. Aaron Burr
says that the great little Madison has asked
to be brought to see me this evening."

After a while, Dolley Todd and James Madison were married. They went to live at Montpelier in Virginia.

Montpelier was a great plantation.

There was a pony for little Payne Todd.

There was a horse for Dolley.

The big house was warmed by great
fireplaces, and lighted by many candles.
Dolley must have remembered a long-ago
time, when she was a little girl on her
father's plantation.

When Thomas Jefferson became President of the United States, he went to the new capital city. James Madison was his Secretary of State.

Dolley and her husband moved to Washington.

The capital city was like a great pond in the middle of a forest.

By day, the wild ducks flew low overhead, and by night, the frogs croaked from the marshes.

When President Jefferson entertained at
the President's Palace, Dolley Madison was
always there. She liked people. She helped
President Jefferson entertain the people who
came there to see him. It made her happy
to see them happy, too.

Now, she wore a white hat with three
long feathers and a beautiful white dress.

When it was time for President Jefferson to leave the President's Palace, the people of the United States chose James Madison to be their president.

The little Quaker girl became the first lady of the land.

Often the President and Mrs. Madison entertained. Dolley found it easy to make other people happy.

"She is always smiling," someone said.

"She is a wonderful hostess," said another.

At this time, the United States and England were at war. English ships sailed into Chesapeake Bay and English soldiers marched to Washington. They set fire to the Capitol building. Other buildings were burning, too —

Dolley Madison was in the President's Palace.

The President was not at home and she waited there for word from him.

While she waited, she wrote a letter.

"I must leave this house," she wrote.

"Where I shall be tomorrow, I cannot tell."

A wagon was brought to the President's Palace. Many things were piled in the wagon. They were ready to leave when Dolley thought about a painting on the wall. It was a painting of George Washington. She would not leave it there.

She waited until the picture was taken
from the wall and sent away for safekeeping.
Then Dolley Madison rode away in her
carriage.

When the English were gone from the city, she came home again. The fires were out, but the walls of the President's Palace were black from the burning.

Dolley Madison and the President moved into a house that had not been burned.

When word came that the war was over, people laughed and cried with happiness.

At last it was time for a new President
to be chosen.

Dolley and James Madison left
Washington. They went to Montpelier.

Here, Dolley and James rode through the green forests together. For many, many years they lived happily on the plantation. Then one day, James Madison died.

Dolley did not want to stay on at Montpelier.

She moved back to Washington.

She lived in a small gray house facing Lafayette Square, across the street from the President's Palace.

The President's Palace had been built again, and painted white. It was now called The White House.

In the Square, horses and cows were tethered, and now and then a pig found its way along the street.

When people came to see the President, they called on Dolley Madison. Her son Payne came often to see her.

Dolley Madison is remembered as a little Quaker girl who went to the President's Palace to live. Perhaps she is remembered most of all for her smile, and for the happiness she always gave to others.

## KEY WORDS

below
bonnet
born
chin
creek
croaked
demurely
died
entertained
evening
fever
free
hostess
important
law
low
marble
married
marsh
mask

often

oysters

perhaps

pine

pirates

plantation

secretly

slaves

sons

speak

spread

tethered

thee

thou

twinkled

vendor

war

wear

wore

### The Author

PATRICIA MILES MARTIN was born in Cherokee, Kansas, and grew up on the prairies of eastern Colorado.

She is married and lives in San Mateo, California, where she devotes all of her time to writing. She has many books for children to her credit, among them are *Mrs. Crumble & Fire Engine No. 7; The Pumpkin Patch; Show and Tell; Calvin and the Cub Scouts,* and *Woody's Big Trouble.*

### The Artist

Recognized as an artist of merit while still in high school, Unada Gliewe exhibited a painting at the Rochester (New York) Memorial Art Gallery. Following graduation from Syracuse University with a major in book illustration, Miss Gliewe worked for several advertising agencies and as the staff artist for the Luthern Board of Parish Education. Her work appears frequently in magazines such as *Jack and Jill.*

The artist makes her home in Philadelphia.